✦ TAROT OF THE DIVINE ✦

Handbook

A GUIDE TO UNDERSTANDING
TAROT SYMBOLISM

✦ *Yoshi Yoshitani* ✦

This handbook belongs to:

_____

Clarkson Potter/Publishers
New York

Welcome

LISTENER,
SPEAKER,
SEEKER

The power of tarot has always run in its rich symbolism. Today, there are agreed upon meanings for each of the seventy-eight cards in a deck, but how an individual decides to interpret the cards before them is where the true majesty of tarot flourishes. This is why each deck, coupled with the unique experiences a reader brings to the table, provides a dizzying and sometimes overwhelming range of possibilities for interpretation. This handbook is here to help.

I created this book to help any tarot reader—from brand-new to experienced readers—form a deeper understanding of tarot. With symbolism breakdowns, unique exercises, and guided ritual suggestions, readers of all experiences will strengthen their understanding of tarot and connection with their intuition.

While my insights are specific to *Tarot of the Divine*, this handbook can be used as a jumping-off point for interpreting the art in your favorite deck. Card by card, you will come to understand the archetypes and symbolism, and by the end of this book you'll have a comprehensive understanding of *Tarot of the Divine* and a broad understanding of tarot as a whole. As you grow and change, so will your perception and intuition. Use the blank space in this book to record your readings, interpretations, and new-found knowledge.

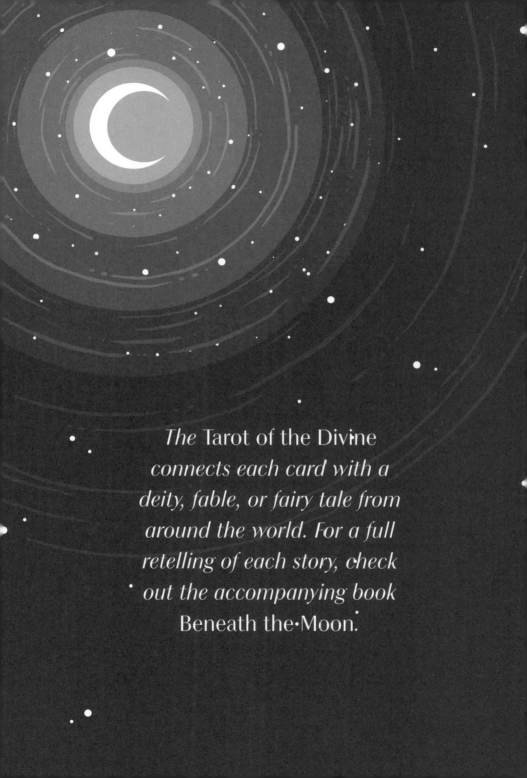

The Tarot of the Divine
connects each card with a
deity, fable, or fairy tale from
around the world. For a full
retelling of each story, check
out the accompanying book
Beneath the Moon.

HOW TO USE THIS HANDBOOK

Symbolism. Relationships. Insight.

We begin with the fundamentals of tarot and the systems they are built on. Alongside a series of card interpretations, you will notice blank pages for your personal use. These spaces are for you to fill with your own insights and experiences.

Document your relationship to a particular card and track your interactions with it. Reference this book during your readings. Record any personal associations you develop as you study the cards. As you fill in these pages, you will develop your own vocabulary and perception of your tarot deck (or decks!). If you completely fill up the pages, feel free to use another journal, or pick up a new workbook and consider how your connection to the cards is constantly evolving.

The last section of this book has pages of exercises, activities, and spreads to help deepen your associations with the cards. You may use these ideas to fill in the card pages of the workbook.

UNDERSTANDING THE TAROT

The tarot is an illustration-driven set of symbols representing different pieces of the universal human experience—the joys, sorrows, excitements, and fears we all face. When these cards are pulled with intention, they can be used to interpret your subconscious, prompt an intuitive response, and connect you to the divine.

Major Arcana

The Major Arcana deals in large archetypes and universal forces. These twenty-two cards represent the larger themes that make up the chapters of our lives and are sometimes called "the Fool's journey." Cards 1 to 21 represent the stages of life and the forces we meet along the way. The Fool, referred to as card 0, travels from a place of fresh wonder to folly, from despair to redemption and, eventually, to a happily ever after when a new journey begins. Many readers choose to use only these cards.

The Fool

The Star

Strength

Minor Arcana

The Minor Arcana is concerned with everyday energies or the small things we regularly encounter. These fifty-six cards represent facets of life that are easier to influence and change. The Minor Arcana can be best understood by exploring the intersection of the suit and numerical meanings found below.

THE SUITS

Cups: Water, emotions, feelings, intuition, relationships
Coins: Earth, physicality, money, career, manifestation
Swords: Air, thoughts, intelligence, communication, truth
Wands: Fire, creativity, inspiration, enthusiasm, energy

Four of Cups

Five of Swords

Six of Coins

Five of Wands

Ace: Beginnings, potential, newness
Two: Duality, balance, cooperation
Three: Groups, movement, expression
Four: Foundation, structure, manifestation
Five: Conflict, challenges, instability
Six: Harmony, alignment, cooperation
Seven: Reflection, introspection, desire
Eight: Rebirth, action, mastery
Nine: Attainment, anticipation, abundance
Ten: Completion, renewal, fulfilment

THE COURT CARDS

Court cards are often associated with a specific person in your life. Each card harnesses the energy of its particular suit (see above), but also carries the additional elemental energy associated with their position in the court:

+ PAGE: The Beginning, Earth, a student: naïve, hopeful
+ KNIGHT: The Action, Air, a champion: opinionated, brave
+ QUEEN: The Heart, Water, a creator: passionate, nurturing
+ KING: The Authority, Fire, a ruler: controlling, structured

Reversals

Reversals add a layer of nuance to your tarot reading. Not all readers choose to use reversals, but those who do interpret the cards' meanings differently if they show up upside down. Reversals can be very personal. Here are a few potential ways to read reversals and remember, follow your intuition—there are no "right" or "wrong" answers.

+ OPPOSITE MEANING: Whatever the upright meaning is, a reversal signals the inverse
+ STUNTED MOVEMENT: You've stayed too long in the position of this card and have begun to ferment
+ EXPLOSIVE ENERGY: An extreme of the upright position, as if its energy has been taken too far
+ PREVIOUS CARD: You have yet to achieve the energy of the upright position—instead, look to the card before it in the deck. For example, if you pull a reversed 6 of Coins, look to the 5 of Coins to find what is keeping you from moving forward

As you start exploring your favorite decks, keep three things top of mind: symbolism, relationships, and insight. Once you have a general sense of the symbolism tied to each card, tarot is all about trusting your personal connections to the cards and your intuition. The rest comes with practice. Take a look at the next page to see how you might interact with this workbook in a personal, visual way. There are more ideas in the Tarot Spreads and Ritual Suggestions section. Use these pages to start your journey—the divine awaits.

Yoshi

The Fool

THE LITTLE MERMAID

The Fool

Naïveté, optimism, adventure

SYMBOLISM

Mermaid. This mermaid—a representation of human and animal duality—wishes to dampen her animal impulse and connect to human consciousness

Red Fish: The drive of pure instinct, passion, and impulse; playfulness

Castle on a Cliff: An unrealized and hazy dream, lifted high on a steep and dangerous cliff; the mermaid can only see her own desires

Water: The realm of the subconscious; the mermaid lifts herself out of the water and into the conscious world to begin her journey

Sun: A blinding hope; bright possibilities

REFLECTIONS

Am I ready to move forward regardless of consequences? How can I be more playful? How might I trust my instincts? What about childhood inspires me? How can I be more open to possibility?

DENMARK

Danish Fairy Tale

◆

The Fool represents a desire to leap into the unknown with joy and abandon.

LAST SEEN
- FEB 15
- MAY 20

I always think about my childhood dog Rascal when I see this card, getting into endless trouble

" If the fool would persist in his folly he would become wise
—William Blake

My Keywords

Elated   Scared

Happy   Nervous

No time
    to question

love seeing
    this card
♥

Major
ARCANA

The Fool

THE LITTLE MERMAID

The Fool

DENMARK
Danish Fairy Tale

◆

The Fool represents a
desire to leap into the
unknown with joy and
abandon.

KEY WORDS

Naïveté, optimism, adventure

SYMBOLISM

Mermaid: This mermaid—a representation of human and animal duality—wishes to dampen her animal impulse and connect to human consciousness

Red Fish: The drive of pure instinct, passion, and impulse; playfulness

Castle on a Cliff: An unrealized and hazy dream, lifted high on a steep and dangerous cliff; the mermaid can only see her own desires

Water: The realm of the subconscious; the mermaid lifts herself out of the water and into the conscious world to begin her journey

Sun: A blinding hope; bright possibilities

REFLECTIONS

Am I ready to move forward regardless of consequences? How can I be more playful? How might I trust my instincts? What about childhood inspires me? How can I be more open to possibilities?

The Magician

THE FAIRY GODMOTHER

The Magician

FRANCE

French Fairy Tale

✦

The Magician represents having everything you need within reach—though you must have the will to grasp it.

KEY WORDS

Transformation, manifestation, power

SYMBOLISM

Fairy Godmother: A creature of immense power who can grant any wish

Wand: Passion, the spark of creativity

Sun and Moon Earrings: Balance, with the godmother at the center of the universe; with one hand lifted to the sky and one closer to the earth, she is a conduit between the divine source and the material universe

White Dress: A purity of intention tinged with blue—perhaps informed by the subconscious

Pumpkins and Mice: The raw materials of the earth, used to transform dreams into realities

REFLECTIONS

What raw materials are at my disposal? What do I want to manifest in my life? What potential lies dormant in the world around me? What actions can I take to make my dreams a reality? What inspires me?

The High Priestess

SCHEHERAZADE

The High Priestess

Wisdom, secrets, intuition

SYMBOLISM

Scheherazade: This storyteller holds all the answers but will only share them indirectly through story, for it is the process of finding answers that makes them worth learning

Book: Knowledge, a higher power; the viewer cannot see what is written, only Scheherazade can

Veil: Mystery, separation, and a distorted view

Moon: Dreams, the subconscious; the crescent moon represents cyclical change

Pillows: Relaxation, letting your thoughts drift into a stream of consciousness

REFLECTIONS

What is my subconscious trying to tell me? What can I interpret from my dreams? Have I encountered any important allegories lately? What secrets am I keeping from myself?

TURKEY
Arabic Folk Tale

◆

The High Priestess represents listening to your subconscious and trusting your heart.

The Empress

OUR LADY OF GUADALUPE

The Empress

MEXICO

Catholic Saint

✦

The Empress represents nurturing motherhood, healing, and a flourishing nature.

KEY WORDS

Fecundity, creation, prosperity

SYMBOLISM

Mestiza: A mother to all, this mixed-race woman represents the merging and unification of multiple cultures

Blessing Hands: A saint revered for her miracles of healing; her gentle hands represent peace, health, and security

Castilian Roses: The Virgin of Guadalupe caused these summer flowers, not native to Mexico, to bloom in winter, symbolizing hope, virility, and abundance

Sun: Warmth, hopefulness; the sun helps plants grow but, like an overbearing mother, can also burn

Tunic and Mantle: The flowery red tunic represents the earth, while the starry blue mantle represents the sky; together they embody the meeting of the mortal and the divine

REFLECTIONS

What do I need to nurture? What will help me grow to my fullest potential? What might I need to heal? How can I be more compassionate to myself or others? Is anything stifling me?

The Emperor

KING ARTHUR

The Emperor

BRITAIN

Celtic Legend

✦

The Emperor represents stability and the protection strong leadership provides.

KEY WORDS

Experience, control, organization

SYMBOLISM

Excalibur: Righteousness, stability, and truth; the sword was lodged in a stone that only the one true king could free

Camelot: The castle King Arthur rules from, where his knights respect his authority

Ram's Head Broach: Aries, the ram—the beginning of the zodiac—symbolizes fiery strength and passion

White Hair: Experience, wisdom

Nature: The scene is well lit and nature thrives, representing mental clarity and fertility

REFLECTIONS

How can I achieve stability? What armor do I need to wear to realize my goals? Am I prepared to defend what I need to? How do I perceive authority? Is there rigidity in my thinking?

The Hierophant
WHITE BUFFALO WOMAN

The Hierophant

NORTH DAKOTA
Lakota Deity

✦

The Hierophant represents a venerated teacher, enlightenment, and structure.

KEY WORDS

Security, tradition, ethics

SYMBOLISM

White Buffalo Woman: A divine figure; a teacher of rules and rituals to live by

Chanunpa: A sacred ceremonial pipe; the *Chanunpa* is presented as an invitation to join White Buffalo Woman's cycle of life and death

Tobacco: A sacred plant often used in ritual offerings and burned in prayer, its smoke traveling from the mortal realm to the divine

Tatanka Skull: Every part of the buffalo is used to support the people and is therefore highly esteemed, representing a fulfilling life lived in observance of the correct cultural tenets

Sacred Hoop: A medicine wheel encompassing all the knowledge of the universe

REFLECTIONS

Who is my mentor? Am I a mentor for someone? Do I find comfort in defined structure? Which traditions do I follow? Which traditions do I wish to overthrow?

The Lovers

THE BEAUTY AND THE BEAST

The Lovers

CHINA

Chinese Fairy Tale

✦

The Lovers represent
choices, relationships,
and duality.

KEY WORDS

Love, union, trust

SYMBOLISM

Beast: Bright red with large horns and
fangs, the beast represents carnality, lust,
strength, restraint, and the element of Fire

Beauty: Dressed in flowing blue,
Beauty represents spirituality, the heart,
emotions, vulnerability, and the element
of Water

Tower: The purple of the tower reflects
harmony and the union between the
lovers, while the flags flutter on the breath
of trusting, passionate communication

Roses and thorns: A flower of love and
romance, the rose embodies beauty that is
difficult to reach amid its thorns; pleasure
and pain

REFLECTIONS

*Am I attracted to someone? Are my
relationships equitable and balanced? Am
I communicating my desires clearly? What
emotional decisions do I have before me?*

The Chariot

THE THREE PRINCESSES OF WHITELAND

The Chariot

NORWAY
Norwegian Fairy Tale

✦

The Chariot represents a clear path—paved by lessons learned—ready to be charged down.

KEY WORDS

Momentum, breakthrough, success

SYMBOLISM

Prince: The Prince's vanity cost him his bride, but he learns from his mistakes and speeds forward to victory, free of petty doubts

Pike Fish: These fish part the waves of the subconscious, their piercing bodies representing clarity of thought

Red Cloak: The cloak represents the power of choice and awareness, with red symbolizing passion, desire, and activity

Fjord: A stretch of water that cuts through steep cliffs far inland, providing quick passage—perhaps straight to the heart

Troll: Catastrophic actions beyond one's control; perhaps an indicator of self-destructive behavior

REFLECTIONS

Where am I headed? What propels me? What obstacles have been cleared for me? How can I claim victory? Is there potential for harm in my rush forward?

Strength

TAM LIN

Strength

SCOTLAND

Scottish Fairy Tale

◆

Strength represents
strength of character,
invincible will, and courage
in the face of fear.

KEY WORDS

Fortitude, conviction, endurance

SYMBOLISM

Transformation: Tam Lin is magically transformed into many terrifying creatures; his lover holds on to him through the dark night, so that he might be rescued from an evil Queen

Monster: Ammit, the Egyptian goddess who ate impure hearts

Crocodile Head: While the power of a crocodile's bite is impressive, its jaws can be kept closed with little force—physical strength is less important than mental fortitude

Oak Leaves: A symbol of endurance and wisdom, the oak tree can live three hundred years and is used to build lasting structures

Dawn: With the coming of dawn there is hope

REFLECTIONS

What are my inner strengths? What fears must I face and overcome? What must I endure? What instincts do I control? Am I allowing others to help me?

The Hermit

DRUID AND WHITE STAG

The Hermit

IRELAND

Celtic Legend

◆

The Hermit represents an inner retreat, a time for introspection and chasing spiritual goals.

KEY WORDS

Self-care, solitude, meditation

SYMBOLISM

Druid: Wise in medical, religious, and judicial matters, druids were often trusted advisors; they were secretive, and many lived as hermits

White Stag: An animal impossible to catch, the stag is a symbol of spiritual enlightenment—the chase itself is its own reward

Dawn: The quiet half-light provides hope and mystery

Forest: Unexplored possibilities of the subconscious mind

Staff: A spiritual leader; a tool used to assist travelers

REFLECTIONS

What do I need to reflect on? Can I benefit from solitary space? Can I take the time to nourish my spirituality? Have I been hiding? Is there something I am chasing for the sake of the chase?

The Wheel of Fortune

ANANSI

The Wheel of Fortune

GHANA

Akan Mythology

◆

The Wheel of Fortune
represents movement
and a swift reversal
in fortune.

KEY WORDS

Luck, karma, change

SYMBOLISM

Anansi: A spider trickster constantly changing the fortunes of those around him, Anansi does not discriminate between villains and heroes

Pot: All the world's stories sat inside this vessel before Anansi released them into the world—like Pandora's box, when this container is opened both chaos and freedom are released

Web: Interconnectedness; if your fortunes are down, it is probably due to past actions

Snake: As snakes shed their skins, they embody rebirth, infinity, and the cyclical nature of life

Fabric: Kente cloth with the pattern meaning "*Obi nkye obi kwan mu si*" (Be kind, as your fortunes might be that of another)

REFLECTIONS

What have I done to change my fortune? What can I do? What do I need to keep moving forward? Am I the trickster? Is someone else?

Justice

AMHAENG-EOSA

XI

Justice

KEY WORDS

Fairness, law, equality

SYMBOLISM

Amhaeng-eosa: Undercover agents hired by the king; they hold the power to dismiss local officials and reward commoners

Mapae: A gold badge used to identify an *amhaeng-eosa*

Geom: A double-edged sword symbolizing both the attacker and the attacked; swords also harken to the suit of swords, representing intelligence and the mind

Taegeuk: The red and blue swirls beneath the *amhaeng-eosa*'s feet represent opposing cosmic forces in balance

Pine Tree: Resilience, honor, strength, wisdom, and dignity

REFLECTIONS

What is out of balance? What needs to be assessed honestly? Is an impartial party needed? What does justice mean to me? Is someone acting unjustly? If there is a decision to be made, what factors need to be weighed?

The Hanged Man
SLEEPING BEAUTY

The Hanged Man

ITALY
Italian Fairy Tale

◆

The Hanged Man represents stasis or a new perspective, maintaining a holding pattern while standing by for better tides.

KEY WORDS
Waiting, peace, reflection

SYMBOLISM

Sleeping Beauty: Cursed to die, the princess falls asleep and her kingdom is blanketed in thorns, waiting for a cure

Orientation: This card looks reversed even while upright, symbolizing a need to look at things from a new angle

Rosebuds: These dormant flowers lie in wait for the right moment to bloom

Valknut Necklace: A symbol of the Norse god Odin, who hung from the world tree for nine days to gain knowledge

Crossed Ankles: A relaxed pose that also precludes movement

REFLECTIONS

How do I find stillness? Can I pause to better analyze my situation? Can I look at the situation in a new way? Am I being distracted? What can I appreciate in this moment?

XIII

Death

WHITE BEAR KING VALEMON

Death

NORWAY
Norwegian Fairy Tale

✦

Death represents the ending
of one way of life, a complete
and irrevocable severance,
and rebirth.

KEY WORDS

Transformation, renewal, devastation

SYMBOLISM

Girl: The transition from child to adult
is a perfect example of the "death" of
childhood

Candle: Illumination in the dark,
enlightenment; the light of a candle
reveals the truth—no matter how ugly

Curtain: The girl has been told not to
look behind the curtain, but is actively
disobedient, perhaps signaling an
independent thinker instead of a blind
follower

Figure: This could be a monster or a
prince—the girl's curiosity triggers an
irrevocable change in her life

Skull: Mortality, consequences,
inevitability, and the pace of time—
that which cannot be stopped

REFLECTIONS

*What phases are ending? What truths
must be challenged? How can I grow? How
am I transforming? What will be missed
and what will be gained with this change?*

XIV

Temperance

BODHISATTVA AVALOKITESHVARA

Temperance

INDIA

Buddhist Bodhisattva

✦

Temperance represents
the balance and
transformation needed to
achieve harmony.

KEY WORDS

Fluidity, moderation, patience

SYMBOLISM

Bodhisattva Avalokiteshvara: The
embodiment of virtue and compassion;
one who has postponed entering paradise
to help every soul in the universe reach
nirvana

Gender: The Bodhisattva Avalokiteshvara
can morph into any gender, age, social
status, or animal to help others obtain
enlightenment

Urna: An auspicious dot on the forehead
symbolizing the third eye; the ability to see
into the divine world

Lotus Pedestal: Rising from murky
waters to bloom, the lotus flower
represents clarity and harmony

Water: One foot in water and one on
land symbolizes a connection between the
emotional and physical realms

REFLECTIONS

*What needs to be tempered? How can
I change to achieve harmony inside
myself? Inside my community? What
needs to be moderated? Can neutrality
be advantageous?*

The Devil

BOITATÁ

The Devil

Temptation, addiction, control

SYMBOLISM

Boitatá: A giant flaming snake that gorged itself on the eyes of the dead until it could see in the dark; greed, gluttony, and wanton destruction; rebirth and transformation

Fire: A symbol of lust; passion that either warms or burns, nurtures or destroys

Forest: The Boitatá is a protector of the forest, especially against those who burn or otherwise harm the trees for selfish reasons

Figures: People who have given into their lusts and face the consequences

REFLECTIONS

Do I have unhealthy connections? What negativity have I kept in my life? When is something too much of a good thing? When do I feel stuck? What can I let go of?

BRAZIL
Brazilian Mythology
✦
The Devil represents obsession with the material world—to the point of harm.

The Tower

RAPUNZEL

The Tower

KEY WORDS

Disaster, revelation, release

SYMBOLISM

Tower: Once a symbol of security and safety, this tower represents hidden weakness

Prince: A man who fell in love with Rapunzel but formulated no concrete plan to save her, he is pushed from the tower and blinded by thorns for his lack of foresight

Rapunzel: A girl hidden in the tower by a witch, she does not plan for her future; she is pushed from the tower and gives birth in the desert, alone

Thorns: The couple falls from grace into a pit of thorns, representing sin, sorrow, and hardship

Lightning: Sudden illumination; a bolt of destructive ignorance

REFLECTIONS

What truths have I been ignoring? What must be acknowledged? Have I perceived someone or something as secure, ignoring hidden weaknesses? Does destruction reveal new freedoms?

The Star

**SISTER ALYONUSHKA AND
BROTHER IVANUSHKA**

The Star

RUSSIA
Russian Fairy Tale

✦

The Star represents
falling to the bottom of the
proverbial well and looking
up with a wish and hope.

KEY WORDS

Faith, regeneration, dreams

SYMBOLISM

Stars: Divine guidance and light in the darkness of the unknown night; eight-pointed stars represent hope and stability radiating from the four corners of the universe

Sister: Even when her brother transforms into a goat, she vows to take care of him, representing unconditional love

White Goat: Purity, good luck, and opportunity; a need to spring forward

Lavender: Purity, serenity, and spiritual healing

Water: Impure water curses Ivanushka, but pure water has healing properties and will cleanse a hero after an ordeal

REFLECTIONS

What am I wishing for? What do I need to heal? What is my guiding light? What am I thankful for in this moment? What are my dreams? Who else is in my constellation?

The Moon

PRINCESS KAGUYA

The Moon

KEY WORDS

Mystery, trickery, trepidation

SYMBOLISM

Tanuki: These raccoon dogs are tricksters in Japanese folklore, constantly donning disguises and hiding their true forms

Multiple Moons: Uncertainty; the reflection of the moon in the water may prompt the question, "Which is the real moon?"

Bridge: A moment where multiple possibilities are connected and a direction must be chosen

Lotus: Clarity blooming from murky waters

Hein Kimono: Women of the Hein court wore many kimono layers to hide their form from prying eyes

REFLECTIONS

What am I not seeing? Am I deceiving myself? Are there choices I must make blindly? What am I afraid of? What do my instincts tell me?

XIX

The Sun

SUN GOD RA

The Sun

EGYPT

Egyptian Deity

✦

The Sun represents optimism, new life, and a world in full bloom.

KEY WORDS

Vitality, happiness, possibility

SYMBOLISM

Sun God Ra: The Egyptian god of creation, responsible for all life; the sun at high noon

Bull's Tail: Worn off the back of a *shendyt*, a bull's tail is a symbol of strength, vitality, and virility

Uraeus: The protective snake goddess wrapped around the disk of the sun, Uraeus represents royalty, divine authority

Water Lilies: Rebirth; this medicinal pain reliever blooms in the sun and closes back up at night

Solar Barge: Ra travels on a solar barge by day, spreading light; each night he traverses the underworld in another barge and is reborn at dawn

REFLECTIONS

What brings me joy? What kind of newness brings me happiness? What rejuvenates me? How can I spread warmth to those around me? How might positive light affect the way I see things?

XX

Judgment

SUN WUKONG, THE MONKEY KING

Judgment

Reckoning, absolution, understanding

SYMBOLISM

Sun Wukong: A trickster monkey who terrorizes heaven, Sun Wukong is stopped by Buddha and put to work learning humility and gaining enlightenment

Circlet: An immovable magical item used to keep Sun Wukong in line, it is removed when he obtains Buddhahood

Buddha: Represented as a lotus in the sky, Buddha is one who has attained bodhi—wisdom in ethical and intellectual perfection

Clouds: Celestial vehicles, clouds are symbols of good fortune and life-giving rain

Mountains: Divinity, perseverance, and great difficulty

REFLECTIONS

Have I learned from past mistakes? Is there a relationship I can reconcile? What am I responsible for? What must I resolve to move forward? What kind of reckoning is on the horizon?

CHINA

Chinese Mythology

✦

Judgment represents responsibility, accountability, and facing the truth to move forward.

XXI

The World

HINEMOA AND TUTANAKAI

The World

NEW ZEALAND
Maori Legend

♦

The World represents spiritual realization and well-deserved happy endings.

KEY WORDS

Wholeness, victory, recognition

SYMBOLISM

Hinemoa: Forbidden to wed her beloved, Hinemoa sneaks out and marries him anyway, representing ultimate fulfillment, satisfaction, and joy

Tutanakai: A solid foundation; Hinemoa can dance with safety and freedom knowing he will catch her

Gourds: Innovation in the face of difficulty; the hollow gourds helped Hinemoa swim to Tutanakai

Kowhai Flowers: Love-fueled miracles, passion, and determination

Sunrise: Hope and possibilities abound

REFLECTIONS

How can I become my truest self? What feels fulfilling? How does it feel to be acknowledged? What does happiness mean to me? Am I ready to move on to my next journey?

Minor

ARCANA

Ace of Cups

MATSUO'S SAKE

Beginnings, celebration, spirituality

Ace of Cups

JAPAN

Japanese Mythology

✦

Ace of Cups represents an outpouring of spiritual, emotional, and creative beginnings.

SYMBOLISM

Nagae-Choshi: A golden vessel used to pour sake in Shinto religious practices, ritual rites, and at weddings; blessings, connection, and unity

Sake: The drink of the gods; bringing people closer to the spiritual world

Sake Barrel: The opening of a barrel, or *kagami biraki*, symbolizes good fortune and harmony

Sakaki Branches: An evergreen tree and sacred space; longevity

Shimenawa: A rope banner with many purposes—purifying, warding against evil spirits, welcoming good spirits— or a symbol of fertility

REFLECTIONS

How can I enjoy this moment? How do I like to indulge? What messages am I receiving from the spiritual realm? Is my cup overflowing? What does that mean to me?

Two of Cups

ENKIDU AND GILGAMESH

Two of Cups

IRAQ

Sumerian Mythology

✦

Two of Cups represents opposites that fulfill each other, drinking deeply of each other's cup.

KEY WORDS

Equality, connection, partnership

SYMBOLISM

Enkidu: Half man, half beast, Enkidu represents the natural world—wild, uncultivated, and innocent—and the human heart

Gilgamesh: Two-thirds god, fully king, Gilgamesh represents civilization, domination, and an insatiable lust. His unending strength is both revered and bemoaned by his subjects

Gold Cup: Enkidu's spiritual ascension

Wood Cup: The true strength found in humility

White Flower Buds: Burgeoning love that hasn't quite blossomed

REFLECTIONS

What does an equal partnership mean to me? How can I uplift someone else? How do I need to be uplifted? Is there someone whose cup I am drinking from? Are they drinking from mine equally?

Three of Cups

APSARA

Three of Cups

CAMBODIA
Hindu Mythology

◆

Three of Cups represents
community celebration
and the joy your
connections bring.

KEY WORDS
Friends, parties, sensuality

SYMBOLISM

Apsara: Celestial beings associated with
the arts, dancing, sensuality, and relaxed
inhibitions; they rule over the fortunes of
gambling

Dancing: Free-spirited Apsara are
always depicted dancing and are known to
fraternize with gods and men alike

Lilies: Flowers that rise from the waters of
emotion represent pure feeling and clarity

Water: The Apsara dance on the surface
of the water, indicating a connection with
their feelings and desires

Banyan Tree: With its ever-seeking
roots, this tree is symbolic of immortality
and fertility

REFLECTIONS

*What brings me joy? What should be
celebrated? How do I feel about
unconventional relationships? Who are
my friends and how can I better connect
with them?*

Four of Cups

THE NIGHTINGALE

Four of Cups

KEY WORDS

Obliviousness, boredom, stagnation

SYMBOLISM

Emperor: A ruler of the material world who covets material goods and forsakes the spiritual creatures that could bring true happiness

Golden Birds: Artifice; these birds represent unfulfilling choices

Nightingale: A visually drab bird possessing a voice beautiful enough to stay death; the overlooked ideal choice

Wooden Chalice: A modest vessel to carry water, its warmth contrasts with the cold metal and gems of the other cups

Peaches: The fruit of the gods; a symbol of divine wisdom and immortality

REFLECTIONS

Am I seeing all possible solutions? Am I coveting the wrong things? Am I wasting my energy? Have I blocked any of my emotions?

Five of Cups

LA LLORONA

Five of Cups

KEY WORDS

Loss, depression, wallowing

SYMBOLISM

La Llorona: Devastated when her husband leaves, she succumbs to her misery and murders her children instead of loving them

Skull: A symbol of death and a celebration of life; La Llorona has her back to the skull, refusing to acknowledge reality

Cups: Though two cups are still full, La Llorona cries over the three spilled in the water instead of celebrating what can be salvaged

Child's Arm: La Llorona weeps with grief, ignoring salvation or judgment even when it reaches out to her

Church: The possibility of redemption

REFLECTIONS

How can I accept loss? What do I despair over? How can I move on? What can I still be thankful for? Is there a reality I am refusing to accept?

Six of Cups

THE SNOW QUEEN

Six of Cups

DENMARK

Danish Fairy Tale

✦

Six of Cups represents idealization of a younger time, using nostalgia to reinvigorate oneself.

KEY WORDS

Memories, innocence, yearning

SYMBOLISM

Kai: A happy child who succumbs to pessimism and goes to live in the Snow Queen's icy realm, symbolizing depression, isolation, and apathy

Gerda: Kai's childhood best friend who journeys to save him, symbolizing hope, congeniality, and affection

Roses: Kai and Gerda's blossoming friendship; the roses that once grew between their windows wilt and die when Kai leaves

Crow: Guidance, movement, and protection; the crow helps Gerda on her journey

Mountain: The Snow Queen's kingdom; personal growth; the friends learn valuable lessons about growing up—they are no longer children

REFLECTIONS

What evokes nostalgia for me? Am I viewing the past too simplistically? In what ways have I grown? What dynamics from the past might be holding me back? How have my friendships evolved?

Seven of Cups

ALADDIN

Seven of Cups

PERSIA
Arabic kimchi

◆

Seven of Cups represents
a multitude of dreams and
fantasies—of which potentially
none are viable.

KEY WORDS

Daydreaming, imagination, wishes

SYMBOLISM

Aladdin: A lazy young man constantly
looking for shortcuts and easy successes

Cave: Secrets, hidden desires, and the
ego of dragon's hoard

Lamps: A high-stakes decision; it is only
possible to select one lamp—the wrong
choice will cause the cave to crumble

Lamp Etchings: A multitude of desires:
the fire of illumination, the hand of
companionship, the peacock of wealth,
the pattern of power, the griffin of wisdom,
the laurel of victory, and the manticore
of supernatural forces

Flowing Water: The passage of time

REFLECTIONS

*What are my current daydreams? How
am I deluding myself? What is the actual
goal I want to achieve? Am I looking for
shortcuts instead of putting in the work?*

Eight of Cups

MOSES

Eight of Cups

EGYPT
Hebrew Legend

✦

Eight of Cups represents
dissatisfaction, the end of
illusion, leaving something that
is no longer fulfilling.

KEY WORDS
Doubt, exhaustion, departure

SYMBOLISM

Moses: Once a prince of Egypt,
Moses becomes disillusioned with the
materialism and selfishness of the court;
he leaves to live a more ascetic life

Ornate Columns: The lavish, overindul-
gent, and vacuous lifestyle Moses leaves
behind

Desert: A retreat into oneself to heal,
choosing spiritual growth

Cups: Moses leaves the cups behind; he
takes nothing with him into the desert,
signifying a complete severance from his
old life

Eclipsed Moon: A journey into the
unknown, the end of one phase and the
beginning of a new one

REFLECTIONS

*What do I feel dissatisfied with? When is
it better to repair and when is it better to
leave? Do I need to change my priorities?
Is something draining my energies? How
can I reignite my passions?*

Nine of Cups

TÀJ AL-MULÚK AND THE PRINCESS DUNYÀ

Nine of Cups

IRAN
Arabic Folk Tale

✦

Nine of Cups represents
happiness brought about in
an unexpected way.

KEY WORDS

Satisfaction, indulgence, abundance

SYMBOLISM

Tàj al-Mulúk: A man whose persistence
eventually wins Princess Dunyà's heart

Princess Dunyà: A woman warned by
an ill omen, one who protects her heart
from hurt

Clothing: Tàj al-Mulúk dresses as a woman
to prove to Princess Dunyà that he will
not betray her; his clothing represents
his sincerity, loyalty, and willingness to
subvert rules and gender roles

Red Dress: Fiery spirit and passion—
which contrasts with Tàj al-Mulúk's
blue headpiece, representing emotional
intelligence

Cups: Victory; rich and decorated, they
are displayed like trophies

REFLECTIONS

*Have my wishes been fulfilled? What
brings me happiness? How has my path
deviated from what I anticipated? How
can I rethink expectations and roles?*

Ten of Cups

JULNAR THE SEA-BORN

Ten of Cups

KEY WORDS

Affirmation, fulfillment, stability

SYMBOLISM

Julnar: A brave and stubborn sea princess
who made the sultan prove and affirm his
love to her before she spoke to him

Baby: The future; a unification between
the land and sea kingdoms, both physical
and emotional planes

Rainbow Arch: Blessings from heaven;
an end to hardships and the start of a
happy life

Mermaid Family: Julnar's family rises
from the sea—a symbol of the unconscious
and dreams—to bless her and her new
family

Roses: Love, passion, desires

REFLECTIONS

*What fulfills me emotionally? Where do
I find joy? What makes me feel secure
and acknowledged? How do I feel about
family? What does a successful family or
chosen family mean to me?*

Page of Cups

BAKUNAWA AND THE SEVEN MOONS

Page of Cups

PHILIPPINES
Filipino Mythology

✦

Page of Cups represents a
dreamer who is fully
connected to his emotions
and spiritual desires.

KEY WORDS

Imaginative, affectionate, intuitive

SYMBOLISM

Young Man: The air of innocence,
expectation, and boundless hope; this moon
took the form of a young man and came to
earth seeking new experiences and loves

Fireflies: Hope, guidance, inspiration, and
awakening; they tell us to follow our hearts

Rabbit: The Chinese god Tu'er Shen who
watches over gay relationships and ties the
red thread of fate between lovers

Sampaguita Flowers: Meaning "I promise
you," these flowers are symbols of love,
purity, and devotion; garlands are often
exchanged between couples

Calm Ocean: Tranquility, peace, spirituality,
emotional balance

REFLECTIONS

*What does my intuition tell me? How can
I embody a young heart? How can I learn
to trust my feelings? How can I purge
negativity?*

Knight of Cups

HALIBU THE HUNTER

Knight of Cups

MONGOLIA
Mongolian Legend

✦

Knight of Cups represents
a kind messenger, someone
who will stand up for
his ideals.

KEY WORDS

Lover, charming, impassioned

SYMBOLISM

Halibu: A generous hunter who supports his entire clan with his skill and kindness

Golden Eagle: A hunting bird and messenger symbolic of strength, courage, independence, and faith

Przewalski Horse: An agile and strong animal; freedom, nurturing, and endurance

Stone: Sacrifice; Halibu surrenders himself, turning to stone to save his clan

Flood: Overwhelming emotion, destruction, a clean slate, renewal

REFLECTIONS

How do I use emotion as a power? What are my personal ideals and how can I better embody them? What message do I need to listen to? Who in my life exudes passion? What feelings drive my actions?

Queen of Cups

YEMOJA

Queen of Cups

KEY WORDS

Empathy, counselor, spirituality

SYMBOLISM

Yemoja: An orisha, or spirit, of rivers and shallow waters, creation, motherhood, pregnant women, fisherman, and those who have died at sea

Cowrie Shells: Sacred to Yemoja and emblematic of great wealth, these shells are used to invoke her protection

Coral: Symbiosis of plant and animal; flourishing coral symbolizes fertility and abundance

Sunbeams: In shallow water, sunbeams shine through, representing a connection between the conscious ground of the earth and the subconscious of the deep ocean

Fish: Yemoja's children, of whom she is fiercely protective

REFLECTIONS

How can I be an empathetic leader? Who in my life is a nurturing counselor? How am I expressing my emotions? How am I working with my subconscious?

King of Cups
THE BOY AND THE DRAGON PEARL

King of Cups

CHINA
Chinese Legend

✦

King of Cups represents a compassionate creature who is a sensitive protector.

KEY WORDS

Generosity, devotion, power

SYMBOLISM

Dragon: Auspicious power and imperial authority (many Chinese emperors claim to descend from dragons); control over water, rainfall, typhoons, and floods

Pearl: An abundant life force that saves the starving boy, turning him into a dragon; spiritual energy, wisdom, prosperity, power, and immortality

Deep Ocean: The vast subconscious—not a place where things grow, but where things are absorbed; tranquility, being fully submerged in patience and wisdom

Crabs: Protection, prosperity, and success; crabs' ability to shed their shells symbolizes rebirth; they may also represent stinginess, cruelty, and insensitivity

Red Mane: The King of Cups is a Fire sign in the suit of Water, so the dragon's passions and emotions are sometimes in conflict

REFLECTIONS

What strengths do my emotions provide? What feelings am I keeping submerged? How can I channel my emotions to my advantage? Am I being overly protective? Who is my protector? How can I support others?

Ace of Coins

JACK AND THE BEANSTALK

Ace of Coins

ENGLAND

English Fairy Tale

✦

Ace of Coins represents new beginnings, financial opportunities, and unexpected prosperity.

KEY WORDS

Cultivation, indulgence, sprouting

SYMBOLISM

Hand: A willingness to act, to build from the ground up

Seed: Undiscovered potential; it is time for this magical seed to be planted

Beanstalk: Fast growing, it presents unexpected rewards for those willing to climb it

Flower Buds: Newly formed, they haven't yet shown their full beauty and fertility

Red Sleeve: A call to follow passions and desires

REFLECTIONS

Have I been gifted with anything recently? What kinds of seeds am I planting? What unexpected opportunities have come my way? Am I making wise investments?

Two of Coins

RHPISUNT

Two of Coins

PACIFIC NORTHWEST
Haida Mythology

✦

Two of Coins represents
duality and the tension
between opposing forces.

KEY WORDS
Balance, priorities, multitasking

SYMBOLISM

Rhpisunt: Carefully juggling her roles
as wife, mother, sister, and provider,
Rhpisunt represents temporary
imbalance and a need for stability

Human-Bear Children: The duality
of nature: continual compromise; being
caught between two worlds

Human Village: Familial obligation,
support, constraint

Bear Cave: Wild passions; impulsivity

Berries: Happiness and love, bounty,
a craving

REFLECTIONS

*Is my financial life in balance with my
desires? Have I overcommitted myself to
anything or anyone? Am I supporting all
aspects of my life appropriately? What
is something I can drop for now and pick
up later?*

Three of Coins
BANJHAKRI AND BANJHAKRINI

Three of Coins

NEPAL
Tamang Mythology

✦

Three of Coins represents apprenticeship, learning from those who came before, and communal support.

KEY WORDS

Collaboration, craftsmanship, learning

SYMBOLISM

Banjhakri: A teacher and god of the forest, he is the connection between the spiritual and mortal realms

Banjhakrini: A bloodthirsty and brutal punisher who reaps students with her sickle

Jhakri Apprentice: A hopeful and sincere youth who takes pride in studying to be a shaman

Dhyangro: A frame drum whose beat is a call to action to join a ritual, prayer, dance, or celebration

Peacock Feathers: Openness, incorruptibility; protection from the Evil Eye

REFLECTIONS

Who can I learn from and what can they teach me? Am I giving myself the time needed to become proficient in my chosen skills? Am I being forced down a path I haven't chosen for myself? How do I respond to adulation? To criticism?

Four of Coins

CONDOR'S WIFE

Four of Coins

KEY WORDS

Hoarding, materialism, avarice

SYMBOLISM

Condor: A scavenger and deceiver, he tricks a human into marrying him

Wings: Wrapping his wings possessively around his prize, the condor is trapped by his own stinginess

Woman· An unwilling wife, oppressed by a husband who is only interested in status

Hummingbird: Cleverness, liberation; the hummingbird helps the woman escape the condor's domination

Cantua Bloom: Unity, hope; following the heart over a duty

REFLECTIONS

Are my desires oppressing others? Where is the line between security and greed? What must I protect? What do I need to let go of? Can I relinquish control of a situation and still feel safe?

PERU

Aymara Folk Tale

✦

Four of Coins represents greed, desire fulfillment, and perceived stability.

Five of Coins

THE LITTLE MATCH GIRL

Five of Coins

DENMARK
Danish Fairy Tale

✦

Five of Coins represents financial misfortune and the denial of support.

KEY WORDS

Destitution, abandonment, hunger

SYMBOLISM

Girl: Naïveté; a girl cut down in the early years of her life, unable to save herself

Matches: Tiny flickers of hope; distractions from the problem at hand

Rags: Inadequate protection; her family has not provided for her, so she is alone with nowhere to go

Snow: Sadness, heaviness, frozen feelings, death

Church: Sanctuary, security; help that feels inaccessible

REFLECTIONS

How does it feel to ask for help? Who can I ask for help? Am I feeling unsupported? In what ways other than materially am I poor? What would make me feel emotionally full?

Six of Coins

THE WOMAN WHO WAS KIND TO INSECTS

Six of Coins

ALASKA
Inuit Fable

✦

Six of Coins represents charity and kindness, the idea of paying it forward.

KEY WORDS

Generosity, patronage, cooperation

SYMBOLISM

Old Woman: Unconditional philanthropy; she frees the insects and chooses to die of starvation rather than eat them

Basket: A gift offered to someone in greater need; openness

Insects: Gratitude, jubilation; unexpected good fortune received

Fox: Good deeds rewarded; karma returning

Mountains: Consistency, firmness, stillness; a connection between the divine and the mundane

REFLECTIONS

How can I support my community? Who am I sharing my resources or abilities with? How can I best mentor someone? Am I giving away too much of myself? What good luck have I received?

Seven of Coins

NANAHUATZIN

Seven of Coins

MEXICO
Aztec Mythology

✦

Seven of Coins represents a decision concerning harvesting: wait for the seed to grow or dig it up to plant something new.

KEY WORDS

Patience, reward, sacrifice

SYMBOLISM

Nanahuatzin: Self-sacrifice, piety, humility; a poor and humble god who willingly self-immolates for the greater good

Tecciztecatl: Self-serving, self-aggrandizing, hesitant; a beautiful and wealthy god who shirks his duties and is punished

Pyre: Death and rebirth; destruction and fertilizer

Sun: The beginning of a new cycle; power, life; a focal point

Maize: A staple crop; a choice

REFLECTIONS

What investments of time or energy have I made? Is now a good time to be patient or cut my losses? What do I need to sacrifice to obtain my goals? What "death" can fertilize new life?

Eight of Coins

SIX SWANS

Eight of Coins

KEY WORDS

Hard work, endurance, determination

SYMBOLISM

Princess: Conviction, dedication; a willingness to endure discomfort

Sores: Pain, potentially permanent damage; a task that causes agony but will reap rewards

Nettles: A grueling and repetitive task requiring skill, resilience, power

Swans: Loyalty, devotion; those who offer loving support, though unable to help directly

Ocean: An endless repetition of tides; freedom on the horizon

REFLECTIONS

What task must I keep pursuing? Will the result be worth the sacrifices? Have I lost my passion for a certain task or activity? Who can I ask for support?

Nine of Coins

THE LEGEND OF THE WATERMELON

Nine of Coins

VIETNAM
Vietnamese Legend

✦

Nine of Coins represents hard work rewarded and benefits reaped, a successful harvest.

KEY WORDS

Self-sufficiency, prosperity, accomplishment

SYMBOLISM

Mai An Tiêm: Clear reasoning, intelligence, cleverness; staying true to your beliefs

Red Clothing: Pursuing projects that engage your passions

Yellow Bird: Good fortune; seizing opportunities; freedom, independence, the ability to travel

Watermelons: Fecundity; a single fruit has many seeds

Boats: Material wealth, stability, and interconnectedness; now living in the center of a trading empire, Mai An Tiêm is supported by a large fleet

REFLECTIONS

How do I relax and enjoy the benefits of my hard work? What opportunities should I seize? What can I accomplish independently? What can I do to trust myself more?

Ten of Coins

PAN HU

Ten of Coins

Abundance, inheritance, quiet

SYMBOLISM

Pan Hu: Loyalty, bravery; having defeated the monster and won the princess, Pan Hu relaxes surrounded by his progeny

Wife: Love and care; a previously troubled relationship is now fulfilling

Pipe: Relaxation and indulgence; luxury; contemplation

Grandchildren: Carefree beneficiaries of work they didn't participate in

Bamboo: Malleable strength, prosperity, luck

REFLECTIONS

In what ways am I wealthy? What traditions are important to me? What am I a beneficiary of? Am I growing complacent in my current situation?

CHINA

Yao Legend

✦

Ten of Coins represents stability—labor that has resulted in peace and security.

Page of Coins

BEAIVI-NIEIDA

Page of Coins

Positivity, innocence, anticipation

SYMBOLISM

Beaivi-nieida: A young sun maiden; the end of seasonal depression; learning new things

Reindeer: Magic, purity; a driving force that keeps moving forward inexorably

Flowers: With new life comes new possibilities; hope, nourishment, medicine

Mountains: A symbol of migration to new pastures, endless movement

Sun: An invigorating warmth and positivity

REFLECTIONS

What new things do I want to learn? Who might need healing and what can I do to help? How do I keep moving forward? What can I grow?

SWEDEN
Sami Deity

◆

Page of Coins represents fresh life, brightness, and a spring in your step.

Knight of Coins

HEITSI-EIBIB

Knight of Coins

SOUTH AFRICA
Khoikhoi Deity

✦

Knight of Coins represents decision making, diligence, and pushing your agenda.

KEY WORDS

Efficiency, ambition, stubbornness

SYMBOLISM

Heitsi-Eibib: A trickster whose practicality has put much of the world together to run effectively; thoughtful, encouraging growth

Ngoni Cow: Heitsi-Eibib's mother who ate magical grass; a stubborn and nurturing symbol of wealth and status

Bow and Arrow: The passing of knowledge; a god of hunting, a teacher of skills

Cairn: Heitsi-Eibib has died many times and come back to life—the cairn represents rebirth, renewal, and learning from past mistakes

Sun: Clear vision, prosperity, vigor

REFLECTIONS

Has stubbornness made me immutable? What is the right balance between being steadfast and flexible? How can I encourage growth in those around me? What is the most practical course of action?

Queen of Coins

WARAMURUNGUNDJU

Queen of Coins

NORTHERN AUSTRALIA
Gunwinggu Deity

◆

Queen of Coins represents
nurturing, caring, and
giving others the tools
to succeed.

KEY WORDS

Brilliance, generosity, advocacy

SYMBOLISM

Waramurungundju: The fertility goddess
and openhanded mother who created
language, nourishment, and enrichment;
her gifts are to be used as the receiver
sees fit

Rainbow Serpent: Fecundity,
menstruation; the duality of life-giving
water and destructive rain

Honeybee Coin: Sweet indulgences,
sexuality, industry, and healing

Moreton Bay Fig Tree: Immortality,
domination

Waratah Flowers: Beauty, visibility,
rejuvenation, healing, protection

REFLECTIONS

*How can I change the elements around me
to better suit my needs? Can I give others
the tools they need to become their best
selves? Am I nurturing myself enough?
What does beauty mean to me?*

King of Coins

HAH-NU-NAH, THE WORLD TURTLE

King of Coins

NORTH AMERICA
Iroquois Mythology

✦

The King of Coins represents stability, assurance, the ability to carry the weight of the world without hesitation.

KEY WORDS

Dependability, success, steadfastness

SYMBOLISM

Hah-nu-nah: All the earth rests on the turtle's back; a physical and financial support; care, endurance

Tree: Longevity; all the seeds of the world come from this tree, and it always has exactly what you need

American Blue Vervain Flowers: Used to cleanse and consecrate ritual spaces, food, and medicine

Cosmos: A consistent, comforting place; an assurance that comes with expectations

Quill-work Necklace: Tradition, sustainability, protection

REFLECTIONS

Who depends on me? Whom do I depend on? Can a slow-and-steady approach help me achieve my goals? Where have I become too set in my ways?

Ace of Swords

GORDIAN KNOT

Ace of Swords

TURKEY
Greek Legend

✦

Ace of Swords represents thinking outside the box and slicing decisively through problems.

KEY WORDS

Clarity, focus, fresh vision

SYMBOLISM

Sword: The penetrating power of intellect; a sharp mind and strong will

Alexander the Great's Hand: An influential visionary, an innovative conqueror

Gordian Knot: An intractable problem easily solved with divergent thinking

Laurel Leaves: Victory; a successful commander

Radiance: Brilliance, attention to a particular moment, intense focus

REFLECTIONS

What brings me clarity? Can I approach my problems from a different angle? What do I need to analyze? What requires bold action?

Two of Swords

SITA

Two of Swords

KEY WORDS

Indecision, stalemate, equilibrium

SYMBOLISM

Sita: Subject to unfair choices, Sita is loyal, strong, and stoic

White and Red Saree: Inner peace, purity, strength, and passion

Khandas: The double-edged swords; a symbol of wisdom cutting through ignorance

Scylla and Charybdis: The sea monster and the whirlpool; feeling trapped between two equally awful choices

Dawn: The shift between night and day; a time-sensitive decision

REFLECTIONS

What choices and options lie before me? What am I closing my eyes to? What decisions am I hesitating to make? What do I need to get through the consequences of my choices?

INDIA

Hindu Epic Ramayana

◆

Two of Swords represents being balanced between difficult choices.

Three of Swords

CRANE WIFE

Three of Swords

KEY WORDS

Heartbreak, self-harm, desolation

SYMBOLISM

Crane Wife: Using deceit to try to help someone you love; she represents small lies that stack up and do great damage

Husband: Breaking his promise to his wife, he represents careless love that can cause pain

Swords: Self-mutilation, harmful words from others, cutting to the heart of the matter

Blood: Life, death, overwhelming feelings, purged emotions

Storm: Chaos, turmoil, depression, trauma

REFLECTIONS

What do I fear within my relationships? What does betrayal mean to me? Am I being honest in my relationships? How might I be emotionally harming myself? What do I regret?

JAPAN

Japanese Fairy Tale

◆

Three of Swords represents betrayal—from an outside force or from an internal struggle.

Four of Swords

FENRIR

Four of Swords

KEY WORDS

Respite, recuperation, reflection

SYMBOLISM

Fenrir: This world destroyer represents strength, destiny, inevitability, destruction, and rage

Gleipnir: This magical gold ribbon holds Fenrir back; the thin thread, protecting the world from carnage, will eventually break and the battle will resume

Mouth Sword: Self-sacrifice for the greater good; foreshadowing defeat

Web of Wyrd Stone: This symbol of the tree of life represents the past, present, and future possibilities; how past and present choices affect the future; and that all timelines are interconnected

Island: Isolation; separate peace

REFLECTIONS

What might I need respite from? What sacrifices can I make to give myself room to recuperate? How can I best gather my strength and restore myself? What battle do I need to prepare for?

NORWAY
Norse Mythology
✦
Four of Swords represents the rest period between battles, the calm eye of the storm.

Five of Swords

OSIRIS, SET, AND ISIS

Five of Swords

KEY WORDS

Duplicity, degradation, violence

SYMBOLISM

Set: The god of chaos, war, and storms; deceit, villainy, and ill-gotten prizes

Isis: The goddess of fertility, magic, and healing; a wronged party seeking revenge

Body of Osiris: The lord of the underworld; the defeated party that the adversary mistakenly believes is exterminated

Horus: The god of kingship and the sky; revenge brought to fruition, the overthrow of a tyrant

Lilies: The sun, rebirth

REFLECTIONS

Am I pursuing my desires ethically? Will there be consequences for my actions later? Am I hurting someone who should be my ally? Have I been wronged by someone or something? What do reparations look like to me?

EGYPT

Egyptian Mythology

✦

Five of Swords represents cruel defeat through illicit means and the potential for revenge.

Six of Swords

DANAË AND PERSEUS

Six of Swords

KEY WORDS

Escape, moving on, healing

SYMBOLISM

Danaë: A princess, once confined, now free; relief after anxieties; rehabilitation

Perseus: A punishment turned into a gift; future possibilities, hope

Chest: A prison turned into a vehicle; movement, a journey

Rough Waters: A tumultuous emotional experience; leaving turmoil behind for the smoother waters ahead

Fertile Land: The future, new growth, potential, abundance

REFLECTIONS

Am I in a situation that is no longer working for me? What should I keep and what should I leave behind? What do I have to look forward to? What do I need to do to heal myself? What gifts have I been given?

GREECE
Greek Mythology

✦

Six of Swords represents leaving a bad situation, hope after abuses, the optimism of a new journey.

Seven of Swords

COYOTE

Seven of Swords

KEY WORDS

Chicanery, manipulation, foolhardiness

SYMBOLISM

Coyote: A trickster god; treachery,
manipulation; being caught in one's
own trap

Shadow: The coyote has many
appearances; disguise, concealed
intentions

Knives: Stolen goods; overwhelming
greed and taking more than one can
possibly carry

Smoke: Destruction left behind; the
possibility of retribution

Forest: Represents being lost,
confusion, illusion

REFLECTIONS

*What schemes are afoot? Are covert
plans taking place without my knowledge?
Am I being tricked or am I tricking myself?
Is there a problem I can solve with an
unexpected solution?*

Eight of Swords

DONKEYSKIN

Eight of Swords

FRANCE

French Fairy Tale

◆

Eight of Swords represents being trapped by one's own insecurities and fears.

KEY WORDS

Paralysis, imprisonment, stagnation

SYMBOLISM

Princess: Safety from a bad situation; the decision to keep hiding in the shadows or to live life once again

Donkeyskin: An ugly disguise to mask the princess's true self—once a salvation, it is now a burden; stitched eyes keep her blind to possibility

Swords: A weapon to pierce the oppressive costume; a need to emerge from a chrysalis

Ring: Liberty, a tentative test of freedom

Castle: An achievable dream, a realized self

REFLECTIONS

What am I holding myself back from? What am I afraid of? What can help me break free of my confines? What possibilities am I not allowing myself to see? How can I know when to act?

Nine of Swords

OEDIPUS

Nine of Swords

GREECE
Greek Mythology

✦

Nine of Swords represents
unrealized fears dominating
one's current situation.

KEY WORDS

Anxieties, nightmares, monomania

SYMBOLISM

Oracle: Diviner of prophecies, represents a warning of what could or will come to pass; nightmares vocalized

Fumes and Vapors: Hallucinogenic trances; potential for substance abuse

King Laius: Actions fueled by terror, causing fears to manifest

Queen Jocasta: A woman motivated by dread, not love; she is denied peace

Baby Oedipus: Intergenerational trauma compounded

REFLECTIONS

What is the source of my anxieties? What nightmares are plaguing me? How are the insecurities of others affecting me? When are my worries effective at protecting me, and when do they hinder me from experiencing my life?

Ten of Swords

SEDNA

Ten of Swords

Betrayal, anguish, nadir

SYMBOLISM

Sedna: Cut off through treachery, she embodies rage, loathing, and hate

Fingers: Sliced off, they became nourishing whales for Sedna, the goddess of marine life; unexpected victories after defeat

Father: The betrayer who harmed his own daughter

Ulu: A heritage knife, symbolizing to be severed from family, cleaved from your past

Water: The subconscious; to drown in turbulent emotions, to wallow in fury

REFLECTIONS

What does betrayal mean to me? What have I been forced to accept? What have I been severed from? How does anger serve me? How does it hinder me? What unexpected new opportunities might be before me?

CANADA
Inuit Mythology

✦

Ten of Swords represents defeat, misery, and being stabbed in the back.

Page of Swords

PRINCESS PARIZADE

Page of Swords

KEY WORDS

Observation, garrulousness, skill

SYMBOLISM

Princess Parizade: A clever and charming diplomat, unruffled by insults

Talking Bird: An advisor and unexpected friend

Singing Tree: Peace, relaxed happiness, enjoyment in what you have

Golden Water: Healing; the problem and the solution

Mosque: An unanticipated windfall from pursuing opportunities

REFLECTIONS

What new opportunities are before me? What unexpected choices could I make to lead to fresh possibilities? Who is an advisor I can listen to? Is there a potential for new friendships? What brings me joy right now?

ANATOLIA
Arabic Folk Tale
✦

Page of Swords represents youth, charm, and a lively, cunning wit.

Knight of Swords

HANG TUAH

Knight of Swords

MALAYSIA
Malaysian Legend

◆

Knight of Swords represents warrior strength, idealism, and a lack of principles.

KEY WORDS

Rational, vigorous, bravery

SYMBOLISM

Hang Tuah: A loyal warrior who achieves his goals through atypical means; the head over the heart

Green, Yellow, and Red: Representative of the Malaysian Islamic faith, royalty, and culture of courage, bravery, and heroism

Taming Sari Kris: A dagger of invulnerability; strength, heroism, fighting spirit, destruction

Horse: Pure intensity of spirit, determination, endurance, intelligence, valor

Melaka Sultanate Palace: Valuing logic and loyalty over emotions

REFLECTIONS

What am I charging toward? What requires my impartial analysis? How can I cut to the heart of the matter? What calls for me to be truthful? When is full honesty harmful?

Queen of Swords

TURANDOT

Queen of Swords

CHINA
Arabic Folk Tale

✦

Queen of Swords represents
ruthlessness and a cold,
analytical enacting of force.

KEY WORDS

Detachment, strategy, protection

SYMBOLISM

Turandot: Retribution, a held grudge;
emotions shaped by logic and intelligence;
cold pursuit of compensation

Peking Opera Headdress: Grandeur,
performance, power

Sword: The executioner's sword is a
symbol of swift justice, sharp rationale

Heads on Pikes: Past adversaries left
as an example to future enemies; those
without a keen mind

Wind: Rapid choices, quick changes,
fast actions

REFLECTIONS

*What are my convictions? How can I
use logic and power to wield my emotions
successfully? Am I being too clinical?
What requires justice? How can I use my
mind to protect what I hold dear?*

King of Swords

GRIFFIN

King of Swords

KEY WORDS

Leadership, impartiality, logic

SYMBOLISM

Griffin: Protection, nobility, wisdom, loyalty

Eagle Half: King of the skies; courage, strength, immortality, honesty

Lion Half: King of the land; authority, leadership, royalty, majesty

Sword: Power, chivalry, domination, justice

Storm: Chaos, swift action, frenetic energy, unstoppable might

REFLECTIONS

What does fair and objective leadership mean to me? How am I using my rationale to achieve my goals? How can I use wisdom to wield power and influence? How can I embody stoic strength?

PERSIA
Persian Mythology

✦

King of Swords represents judgment, wisdom, and power, an emotionally distant intelligence.

Ace of Wands

THE MAGIC PAINTBRUSH

Ace of Wands

KEY WORDS

Inspiration, empowerment, excitement

SYMBOLISM

Brush: A tool that can bring anything to life; infinite possibilities, hopes, dreams come true

Flame: Passion and ambition; desire, willpower

Peonies: Regarded as the king of flowers, the peony represents honor and prosperity, bravery, love, and good luck

Bamboo: Moral integrity, loyalty, beauty

Shining Light: A sign of life, a beginning; celebration, divine inspiration

REFLECTIONS

What inspires me? How do I express myself creatively? What passions motivate me? What ignites my imagination? What principles ground me? What makes me feel empowered?

CHINA

Chinese Folk Tale

✦

Ace of Wands represents the creative potential right before the ink hits the paper—a spark.

Two of Wands

JANUS

Two of Wands

ITALY
Roman Mythology

✦

Two of Wands represents planning, travel, and crossing a threshold to a new adventure.

KEY WORDS

Decisions, cooperation, opportunity

SYMBOLISM

Janus: The two-headed god of doorways and transition; a symbol of progress informed by the past

Staff and Key: Together they symbolize travel and the ability to open any door; potential, connection, exploration

Grapes and Wine: Hand-crafted offerings, connection; celebration

Laurel: A well-known symbol of victory; recognition of achievement

Harbor: Commerce, trade, and merchandise; journeys

REFLECTIONS

What do I plan to accomplish? What exciting challenges do I face? As I stand on this threshold, what can I see both before and behind me? What is currently in transition? Do I need to travel to find more opportunities?

Three of Wands

THE ENCHANTED PIG

Three of Wands

KEY WORDS

Progress, self-motivation, aid

SYMBOLISM

Princess: Forced out of her comfort zone, she takes control and faces challenges head-on; self-assurance

Bone Ladder: Accepting help from others; allies

Missing Pinkie Finger: Sacrifice made to reach a goal

Three Wands: A long journey, many roads traveled

Castle: The previously unattainable now within reach

REFLECTIONS

What are my ambitions? Has my path deviated? What are my dreams for the future? What help should I accept? What sacrifices am I willing to make to achieve my goals?

ROMANIA
Romanian Fairy Tale

◆

Three of Wands represents the personal confidence and outside assistance needed to reach goals.

Four of Wands

MOHINI AND ARAVAN

Four of Wands

INDIA
Sanskrit Epic Poem

◆

Four of Wands represents
a celebration of happiness
before the next challenge.

KEY WORDS

Rejoicing, community, warmth

SYMBOLISM

Mohini: The god Krishna's female form
represents transformation, joy, bliss, and
commitment

Aravan: Indulgence before sacrifice;
fully enjoying the moment

Mandap: A canopy lifted by four pillars,
symbolizing security, sanctity, and support
from the community

Garlands: Good luck, success, prosperity,
happiness

Jaimala: Garlands exchanged to indicate
an accepted marriage proposal; happiness,
excitement, and beauty

REFLECTIONS

*What challenges have I overcome?
How can I celebrate? Am I enjoying my
successes with my community? Who
supports me through trials and victories?
How can I restore myself to prepare for
the next project?*

Five of Wands

THE PANDAVAS

Five of Wands

INDIA
Sanskrit Epic Poem

✦

Five of Wands represents the opposing tensions of rivalry, conflict, and unity.

KEY WORDS

Competition, disputes, opponents

SYMBOLISM

Smiles: The five brothers are rivals, but they are at their strongest when united for a common cause

Yudhisthira: A unifying force who is also responsible for fragmenting relationships between his brothers; justice, righteousness, truth; gambling as weakness

Bhima: Strength, vitality, willpower; ruthlessness as weakness

Arjuna: Courage, focus, purity; pride as weakness

Nakula: Beauty, loyalty, unity; narcissism as weakness

Sahadeva: Compassion, wisdom, foresight; arrogance as weakness

REFLECTIONS

What games am I playing? How do I feel about competition? What can I learn from conflict? How do I relate to my rivals? How do I present my ideas to others? Are there opportunities for alliances?

Six of Wands

YENNENGA

Six of Wands

KEY WORDS

Achievement, praise, recognition

SYMBOLISM

Yennenga: A princess warrior and commander who forged her own path; rebellion, courage, strength, proficiency

Horse: A creature with determination, endurance, and valor; freedom

Spears: A swift and powerful skill; directness, honor

Wheat: Fertility, abundance, prosperity; future security

Fire: A severing of ties; war, change

REFLECTIONS

What victories can I acknowledge? Have I defeated something? What are my strengths and skills? What decisive actions can I take next? What do future victories look like to me?

Seven of Wands

JOHN HENRY

Seven of Wands

KEY WORDS

Struggle, fidelity, resolve

SYMBOLISM

John Henry: A freed slave and figure of strength and endurance, exploited labor, and the dignity of humankind; fighting against the impossible for what is right

Hammer: Symbol of the working-class hero, justice, and might

Steel Drill: Hammered into rock to make space for dynamite; a concentrated force, honed intent, focus

Train: The machine age, technology, innovation

Mountain: Order, firmness, durability

REFLECTIONS

What beliefs do I hold on to even under pressure? Who or what am I up against? Is the fight in front of me part of a larger battle? Where do my loyalties lie? What results am I hoping for? How can I effectively promote my point of view?

ALABAMA

American Folk Tale

✦

Seven of Wands represents indomitable will, standing up for one's beliefs.

Eight of Wands
RAINBOW CROW

Eight of Wands

Eight of Wands

KEY WORDS

Speed, travel, intention

SYMBOLISM

Crow: A sacrifice of colorful plumage that brings life-saving fire to the cold Earth; martyrdom; investing in community

Fire: A burning symbol of life, hope, creativity, nurture, and nourishment; often viewed either as a gift from the gods or as stolen from immortals

Flight: A vacation or trip; fast, direct activity; motion

Snow: Stagnation or stillness; frozen actions

REFLECTIONS

Where do I want to go? What has been suspended that I want to bring action to? Is there a need for quick decision making? What sacrifices will be made with swift action? What can be gained from focus?

NORTH AMERICA
Lenape Legend (Disputed)

✦

Eight of Wands represents decisive actions and swift movement.

Nine of Wands

VASILISA THE BEAUTIFUL

Nine of Wands

RUSSIA
Russian Fairy Tale

✦

Nine of Wands represents
persevering through fatigue.

KEY WORDS
Defense, tenacity, resilience

SYMBOLISM

Vasilisa: Put through a list of impossible
trials, she is still polite and kind; steadfast
ness, loyalty, purity, truth

Doll: Selflessly cared for by Vasilisa,
it saves her in return; reciprocity, aid,
familial love

Skull Fence: Past failures; a warning to
stay true to your convictions

Baba Yaga: A powerful figure of mixed
morality; an unpredictable authority

Gladiolus Flowers: Strength of
character; faithfulness, sincerity, and
integrity; never giving up

REFLECTIONS

*What opposition am I facing? Am I
anticipating something? What gives me
strength when I face difficulties? Where
can I find support? How can I stay kind
while under pressure?*

Ten of Wands

TIMBO TREE

Ten of Wands

Overwhelm, obligation, drowning

SYMBOLISM

Saguaa: A father searching for his daughter alone; overwork, shortsightedness, anxiety; a rejection of support

Skull: Death, mortality, burnout; rebirth

Timbo Tree: Growth and resurrection; protection, commitment, duty

Timbo Fruit: Though the father's ears are still listening for his daughter, the fruit of his sacrifice can only be enjoyed by others

Orchids: Beauty, love; the missing daughter, the unattainable

REFLECTIONS

Am I taking on too much? Am I allowing others to eat the fruits of my labors? What responsibilities are weighing on me? Can I split up my burdens among those who would help me?

PARAGUAY
Guarani Legend

✦

Ten of Wands represents taking too much responsibility and refusing assistance.

Page of Wands

MWINDO

Page of Wands

KEY WORDS

Enthusiasm, playfulness, cleverness

SYMBOLISM

Mwindo: A magical child, clever and determined; carefree with youthful insight and infinite creativity

Scepter: A flyswatter made of a buffalo tail; power, magic, potential

Adze: A cutting tool symbolic of the harvesting cycle; creation, fertilization, energy

Bananas: An impossible task achieved; miracles, vitality, new life

Red Clothing: Confidence, passion, courage, and adventure

REFLECTIONS

What new endeavors bring me joy? What am enthusiastic about? What lights my inner flame? What new things do I want to create? Where can naïveté benefit me? How can I change the world around me?

Knight of Wands

TATTERHOOD

Knight of Wands

NORWAY

Norwegian Fairy Tale

◆

Knight of Wands represents
a daring fighter, a rebellious
flirt, and a hot-headed rebel.

KEY WORDS

Adventure, charisma, spirit

SYMBOLISM

Tatterhood: A temperamental child of
passions; her cloak flares out like a flame;
unbridled intensity, ferocity, loyalty, pride

Goat: Sure-footedness, creative energy,
vitality, and health

Spoon: An object to hold the waters of the
subconscious; a dominant force, power in
the unexpected

Cow Head: The head of Tatterhood's
compliant sister, silly, submissive, and sweet

Boat: Traveling to pursue desires; a journey

REFLECTIONS

*How do I fight for my passions? What
do I lust for? How can I wield my skills in
new and unexpected ways? What should
I charge toward? What risks am I taking?
How can I continue to grow?*

Queen of Wands

PELE

Queen of Wands

HAWAII
Hawaiian Deity

✦

Queen of Wands represents
the nourishment and
destructive force of an
open flame.

KEY WORDS

Passion, heat, confidence

SYMBOLISM

Pele: Goddess of volcanos and fire,
creator of the islands of Hawaii, Pele
represents majestic power, capriciousness,
volatility, and innovation

Pa'oa: Used to pull potential from
the earth, this stick is a source of both
divination and destruction

Lei: An emblem of respect, power, and
influence

Ohia Lehua: The first plant to grow
out of fresh lava, its flowers represent
determination, renewal, and fertility

Volcano: An upheaval; creation through
destruction; released emotions

REFLECTIONS

*What gives me the energy to create? How
do my passions drive me? How can I use
my vitality to invigorate those around me?
When can jealousy be useful and when is
it harmful? What potential can I pull from
the opportunities around me?*

King of Wands

THE PHOENIX

King of Wands

KEY WORDS

Authority, boldness, magnetism

SYMBOLISM

The Phoenix (Eastern Tradition):
Divine power, nobility, loyalty, honesty,
auspiciousness, and high virtue

The Phoenix (Western Tradition):
Immortality, resurrection, faith, passion,
and overcoming challenges

Firebird Feathers: Pursuit of desires;
illumination, warmth

Fire: Wisdom and hope; death and rebirth

Sun: A clarifying life force and energy;
positivity, confidence

REFLECTIONS

*How can I effect transformation? How can
my power protect those around me? What
needs to die for something to grow? Does
my power smother?*

This section of your handbook provides some rituals suited to support your understanding of tarot and build your relationship with your favorite deck. Use the space provided in the previous section to log any important discoveries, surprising readings, or striking learnings to assist in your journey.

Tarot Spreads

AND RITUAL SUGGESTIONS

It's important when doing any tarot reading—from single card pulls to complex, multiple card spreads—to have a specific intent. Meditation is a great way to clear your mind and hone in on a question you want to ask your deck.

For example, if you're hoping for a reading about your career but you can't stop thinking about your romantic life and what you're going to eat for dinner and a thousand other things happening in your life, your reading will be equally muddled. Is this reading about your career or about your love life?

There are many ways to meditate and there is no *wrong* way—as long as it serves you. Here are a few recommendations . . . find one that works for you!

+ Take several slow, deep breaths while focusing on your question
+ Shuffle the deck for as long as you need to clear your mind
+ Listen to music before or during your reading to help soothe you
+ Practice some full-body stretches to expel unnecessary thoughts
+ Light a candle and mindfully focus on its fragrance
+ Draw a picture with no intentions or color in a coloring book
+ Run your hands repeatedly over a tactile surface like fur, wood grain, leather, or crystal
+ Ritually cleanse your deck—this is as much a cleansing of your mind of negativity

THE DAILY DRAW

A wonderful way to become familiar with your deck and tap into your intuition is with a daily draw. You can pull a single card first thing in the morning or as the last thing you do before bed.

For a morning reading, clear your mind shuffle your deck, and pull a single card. Consider this card as your intention for the day. What thoughts show up? What positives do you see? What negatives do you see? Reflect on what this card means for you and keep it close throughout the day.

For an evening reading, clear your mind, shuffle the deck, and pull a single card. Consider this card a representation of the day you just had. What thoughts show up? Does this card make you think of a person, situation, or an event from the day? Why? Open up to your subconscious. Let it help your conscious mind process the day and what it meant to you.

Keep track of your daily draws. Write down which day you pulled a particular card and reflect on your reading. Are there cards that seem to show up frequently? Do you notice repeating themes in your life? What does your intuition seem to be guiding you toward? Continue to make personal connections to better understand your deck.

THE THREE-CARD SPREAD

The best way to learn tarot is through practice. Read for yourself and read for friends! As long as you have a clear intention in mind before you pull cards, it's okay to ask really silly questions, too. Remember to always do a quick mind-clearing meditation before you start a reading.

Three-card spreads are easy to get the hang of, but don't be fooled! They offer deceptively deep insights and cut right to the heart of the matter. A trio of cards can shed light on a multitude of inter- and intrapersonal interactions. Again: you can ask anything of your deck as long as you are clear on what you want these cards to represent.

If there is ever a card that mystifies you, pull one more card and place it on top of the confusing card, asking your deck for clarification.

Here are some meanings to assign the cards in a three-card spread:

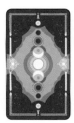 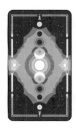 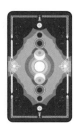

For a general reading:

Past	Present	Future
Tomorrow	Next week	Next month
Mind	Body	Spirit
Strengths	Weaknesses	Advice
Where am I under-performing?	Where I am over-committing?	How can I achieve balance?

For a specific situation or challenge:

A goal	A blockage	How to overcome
What worked	What didn't work	What I learned
Option 1	Option 2	How to make the best decision

For a specific relationship:

You	Another person	The relationship
What you want	What they want	Where you're both headed

THE FIVE-CARD SPREAD

Five-card spreads offer layers of complexity. Look out for relationships among cards and any patterns that begin to appear. Spreads with lots of coins, for example, can indicate a financial or material need or challenge. Multiple cards with Water may speak to the importance of dreams or the subconscious.

In this example spread, the reader may ask a goal-oriented question like, "How can I improve my relationship?" or "How can I get a raise?" or "How do I complete this project?"

1. THE SITUATION: This card represents the current circumstance
2. CHALLENGES: What are the difficulties keeping me from my goal?
3. AIDE: Who or what is helping me reach my goal?
4. HIDDEN INFLUENCES: What is affecting me that I am not consciously aware of?
5. ADVICE: This card represents next steps toward achieving your goal

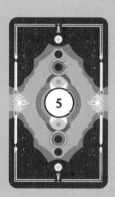

Advice

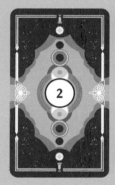

Challenges

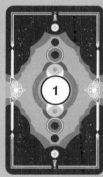

The situation

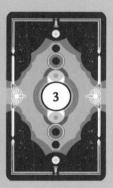

Pride

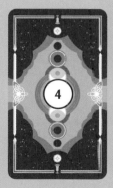

Hidden influences

THE CELTIC CROSS: A TEN-CARD SPREAD

This popular tarot card spread can be used to look at the broad scope of a particular situation. Focus on a clear intention, such as "my romantic life," "my career," or "my family." As always, clear your mind, focus on your intent, and look for patterns in the cards.

Major Arcana cards are considered a more potent intense energy and usually mean special attention should be paid to where they are placed. Spreads with many Major Arcana cards may indicate strong forces at play and an important decision to be made.

1. THE SITUATION: The present state of things
2. CHALLENGES: What are the problems at hand?
3. NEAR PAST: What happened recently?
4. NEAR FUTURE: What will happen next?
5. THE GOAL: What would you like to achieve?
6. THE ROOT: What has caused this current situation?
7. SELF-PERCEPTION: What does your internal energy indicate? What is your point of view?
8. ENVIRONMENT: What does the energy of your surroundings indicate? What outside forces are at play?
9. ADVICE: What should be done?
10. POTENTIAL OUTCOME: Where the situation could lead

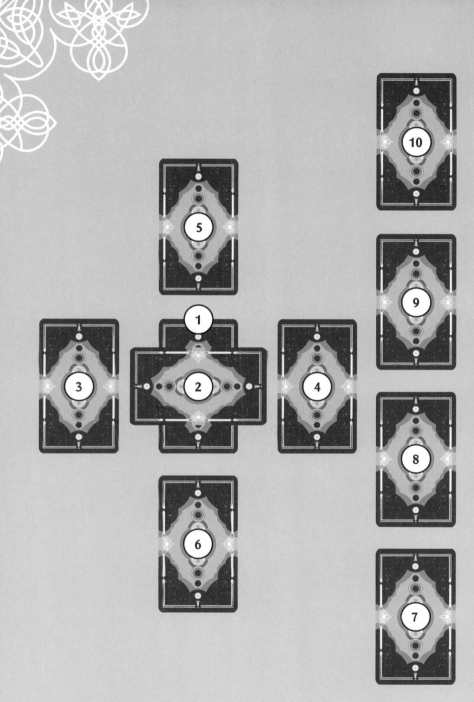

THE YEARLY SPREAD

This is a great spread to perform at the beginning of a year or on a birthday, but it can be done at any time. It may appear large and intimidating, but is a great way for advanced readers and beginners alike to flex their tarot-reading muscles.

Be on the lookout for card patterns; they usually indicate something that needs to be paid especial attention to, or a reoccurring challenge.

- ✦ CARDS 1 TO 12: Starting with the current month, pull a card to represent the themes of the twelve months to come
- ✦ CARDS 13 TO 16: Each of these cards represents themes of the four seasons or quarters in a year. Each quarter card will interact with three-month cards.
- ✦ CARD 17: Advice for the year
- ✦ CARD 18: Theme for the year
- ✦ CARD 19: Challenges for the year
- ✦ CARD 20: Your guide for the year. This card is placed sideways because it embodies the positive and negative aspects of the card and must be interpreted as such.

Can be done at any time, with any deck, starting with card 1 as the current month.

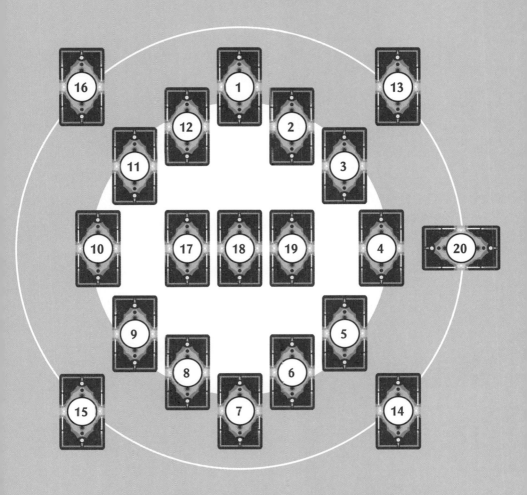

1.	January	8.	August	15.	3rd Quarter
2.	February	9.	September	16.	4th Quarter
3.	March	10.	October	17.	Advice
4.	April	11.	November	18.	Theme
5.	May	12.	December	19.	Challenge
6.	June	13.	1st Quarter	20.	Guide
7.	July	14.	2nd Quarter		

CREATE YOUR OWN SPREAD

While there are many accessible spreads to try, sometimes it's hard to find one that works for you and for the question you are pondering. It can be useful (and lots of fun!) to make your own spreads.

Here's how I create my own spreads:

1. WRITE POSITIONS ON INDEX CARDS: Look for spreads online or in your favorite tarot books and write down the positions that speak to you (such as past, challenges, situation, goals) on separate index cards. Add positions of your own as they occur to you. Keep riffing until you have a nice pile.

2. THINK OF YOUR NEEDS: Focus on your intention or question and the kind of information you'd like to receive. Do you need to weigh two options? Do you need to know the consequences of an action? Do you need to understand your own feelings? How many cards would you like to pull? Small spreads are short and concise, while larger spreads can take a while to unpack.

3. CRAFT A SPREAD: Lay out your index cards. Consider the shape you make—you can make a line or a heart or a cat face. Consider symmetry—a good question is balanced with pairs, like cause and effect or past and present. Once you settle on a spread, set the rest of your index cards aside.

4. TEST THE SPREAD: Shuffle your deck, ask your question, lay out your cards, and do a reading.

5. RECONFIGURE AS NEEDED: If the spread didn't meet your needs or didn't feel right for any reason, swap out index cards and change the layout as you see fit. Be sure to save all your index cards for the next time you want to make a new spread . . . and share your spread with all your friends!

PERSONAL EXPERIENCES

Understanding tarot goes hand in hand with building personal connections to the cards. For this exercise, start by clearing your mind and shuffling your deck. Randomly pick a card and study its meaning.

Consider one or all of the following questions:

+ How can this card be applied to my personal life?
+ Is there a time in my life that reminds me of this card?
+ Is there a time when I would have benefitted from the advice on this card?
+ Does this card remind me of someone else's life?
+ Is there an historical event that parallels this card? What about a scene from a movie or book?

If you can think of multiple connections, that's great. Write down your thoughts and keep updating your notes as time goes on.

THE TAROT SCRAPBOOK

Start by clearing your mind and shuffling the deck. Randomly pick a card and study its meaning. Using a blank page in this book (or a separate journal or sketchbook), decorate the page with things that remind you of that card. This exercise will enhance your studies by allowing you to build personalized visual cues for each card, solidifying your understanding of the themes in tarot. Plus, it's fun to show off your results!

Some material suggestions:

+ Stickers
+ Washi tape
+ Pictures of friends, printed news articles, or screenshots

- ✦ Pressed flowers
- ✦ Origami
- ✦ Famous quotes
- ✦ Magazine cutouts
- ✦ Stamps
- ✦ Paints, colored pencils, crayons, watercolor, markers
- ✦ Scraps: movie tickets, candy wrappers, receipts
- ✦ Diary entries

If you choose to use this handbook as a scrapbook, I'd encourage you to work on each card's page bit by bit. Every time you do, meditate on the card and its meaning. Don't worry about filling it in all at once, either. Leave yourself room to grow and explore.

MUSIC ASSOCIATION

Randomly pick a card and study its meaning. Spend some time finding a song that evokes the card's essence. It can be any song, from a children's rhyme to a classical piece, or indie, rap, or pop music. It doesn't matter if it makes sense to anyone else, as long as the association makes sense to you. If you are having a difficult time, read about the card again and pull out a specific insight that resonates with you. Use that as a starting point.

Flip to the card's page in this workbook and record some of your favorite lyrics while ruminating on the card. Perhaps write down some of the reasons you chose the song and anything you know about the artist or album. Periodically play the song while meditating on the meaning of the card. Over time, your association between the two should become stronger.

Repeat until you've gone through every card in the deck.

CELEBRITY MATCHUP

This is a great exercise for the court cards and much of the Major Arcana. Think of your favorite historical figures, acquaintances, or fictional characters and consider which tarot card they most embody. In what ways does your chosen figure exemplify the characteristics of the card you chose? Do they epitomize the positive or the negative aspects—or both? You may choose to draw a picture or glue in a photo of your figure. Now whenever you draw this card, think to yourself, "What would this figure do?"

They don't have to be famous or even human! Here are some potential icons to explore:

+ Celebrities
+ Historical figures
+ Friends or relatives
+ Monsters
+ Animals or pets
+ Plants
+ Fictional characters from TV shows, movies, comic books, anime, or role-playing games

Over time, you might notice your perceptions change when you come back to the card. Does the association still work? Have your thoughts on the figure or card evolved in new ways? Consider how two "celebrity" cards interact when pulled together. Do any cards show up together in readings often? Why do you think that is?

THE POSITIVE AND THE NEGATIVE

This exercise will help you explore the relationships between positive and negative meanings and relationships, both in the deck and within yourself.

To begin, divide the deck by pulling out all the cards that feel "negative" to you. There are no right or wrong answers—trust your intuition. Study the "negative" cards one by one and consider their meanings. What makes each card undesirable? Is there a "positive" interpretation? In what situations might this "negative" card be good? Have you seen a time when this card meaning was beneficial?

After you've explored your "negative" associations, do the same exercise for the cards you deem "positive."

By exploring the duality of each card, you'll create a flexible understanding of the tarot, giving you a better grasp of nuance in larger spreads.

GOAL SETTING

This exercise strengthens the connection between tarot and your daily life, while also serving as a tool to help you set and achieve personal goals. Set an intention for yourself. It can be something small or large in scope.

Here are some questions to guide you:

+ What goal would I like to accomplish this week? This month?
+ What theme should I give myself this year?
+ What should I channel in this upcoming conversation?
+ What kind of friend do I want to be?
+ What do I desire romantically?
+ What do I want for my career?
+ What do I need to get through this project?

Once you have a clear intention or question in mind, flip through the deck and find a card that matches your desires. Place it somewhere easy for you to see and refer to throughout the day. Channel its energy whenever you feel stuck.

CARD PAIRING

Tarot cards are powerful on their own, but they offer nuanced insight when paired together. This is a simple exercise to build on the connections you've already made while strengthening your understanding of the cards as they interact with each other.

1. PICK A CARD. Start with one you connect with or one that's giving you trouble.
2. SIMPLIFY THE CARD'S INTERPRETATION INTO A SINGLE NOUN, for example: student, woman, friend, mystery, or heartbreak.
3. PULL A SECONDARY CARD AND SIMPLIFY IT INTO AN ADJECTIVE, for example: lively, wanton, sad, or accomplished.
4. USE THE SECONDARY CARD TO MODIFY THE FIRST CARD. Together, they offer a more specific noun, for example: frivolous child, mischievous interloper, or joyous darkness.
5. CONTINUE TO REPLACE THE SECONDARY CARD and go through the rest of the deck in this manner. The whole process should be quick and impulsive. Follow your gut.
6. RECORD YOUR FAVORITE COMBINATIONS AND REFLECT on the associations you've made.

7. **REPEAT STEPS 1 THROUGH 5 FOR THE REST OF THE DECK.**
   (Don't feel the need to do it all in one sitting!)

Once you feel more confident in the cards, you can start moving on to more complex connections. Start examining the differences, similarities, and visual interactions between pairs (and even among trios) of cards in your favorite deck.

CREATE A STORY

Many writers and creators find tarot as a great idea generator or creative block buster. A tarot reading can be a gateway to writing stories, designing characters, or forming a world. Focus on an intention and then pull your cards. Allow the meaning of the card or the artwork itself to inspire you.

Use these prompts to create something specific or as a fun activity to perform with friends:

+ Pull a single card when you're unsure what to write next
+ Pull three cards for your plot, conflict, and the resolution of a story
+ Pull three cards to be a character's strength, critical flaw, and motivation
+ Pull four cards to determine what lies North, South, East, and West of a location
+ Pull five cards to be the who, where, when, problem, and solution of a story

. . . or create your own prompts—just make sure you set a clear intention and plan what each card will mean before you pull!

SAMPLE JOURNAL TEMPLATE

As you've learned by now, the best way to understand tarot is with experience. Keep a journal of your readings—record your interpretations and reflect on patterns, changes, or growth over time. The more you work with your deck, the more your understanding and intuition will flourish.

Here is how I record my readings. Use this template in the pages of this book or in a special journal designated for your tarot work.

Question:	
Spread:	**Date:**
	Keywords:
	Feelings:
Interpretation:	
Reflection:	

Keep track of some of your favorite tarot books, websites, or decks here.

Published in the United States by Clarkson Potter/Publishers, an imprint
of Random House, a division of Penguin Random House LLC, New York.

ClarksonPotter.com
RandomHouseBooks.com

CLARKSON POTTER is a trademark and POTTER with colophon is a
registered trademark of Penguin Random House LLC.

Artwork based on *Tarot of the Divine* (Clarkson Potter, 2020).
Copyright © 2020 by Yoshi Yoshitani.

Editor: Sara Neville
Designer: Danielle Deschenes and Lise Sukhu
Production Editor: Serena Wang
Production Manager: Luisa Francavilla
Composition: Dix Type
Copy Editor: Alison Hagge
Marketer: Chloe Aryeh

ISBN 978-0-593-23654-3

Printed in Malaysia

10   9   8   7   6   5   4   3   2   1

First Edition